Main Street Marketing 3.0
For Local Business Owners

Use Personal Branding To
Stand Out From Your Competition and
Skyrocket Your Earnings

Leon E. Spencer

Main Street Marketing 3.0 for Local Business Owners

CONTENTS

Introduction

Congratulations for taking the first steps in growing your business and creating your personal brand using Social Media. You obviously are interested in implementing some of the best marketing strategies known today and Personal Branded Marketing will take you there.

What you are about to discover, since a *major change* has taken place within traditional advertising and marketing, is a way to stand out from your competitors while growing your business. With what I like to call, Personal Branded Marketing, you can utilize social media and content marketing as an affordable option to create a personal brand and blow the doors off your competition.

In fact, from large corporations to small one person home-based businesses, Personal Branded Marketing is changing the way that marketing is done.

One of the best elements of this new trend is that most of this type of marketing can be free and has been proven to work as well, *if not better*, than traditional marketing strategies!

If you take the time to learn and implement Personal Branded Marketing strategies, you can quickly and effectively change your financial future.

You will be able to make *more* money, *more* quickly and *more* efficiently than ever before.

This book will give you specific tools, techniques, tips, and ideas for your business that you can implement *immediately* for instant results. You'll also learn how you can help your clients with their social media as well.

You are going to receive in-depth knowledge of proven Personal Branded Marketing techniques and strategies to effectively launch a dynamic marketing campaign without spending a lot of money!

Follow what is outlined in this book carefully, and you will undoubtedly have a strong understanding of the underlying philosophy of Personal Branded Marketing as well as an exact plan on how to begin utilizing some of the most powerful marketing platforms available to you and your business today.

You are going to learn how to put your resources to work so that you increase your profits and save an incredible amount of time and money.

OK...Let's get your journey started into the world of Personal Branded Marketing. Once you discover this world, you will never, ever turn back!

Before we get started, let me take a minute to tell you a little about my background. At a very young age I realized that I enjoyed business and marketing. As a young kid, my Mom was an Avon lady and I enjoyed coming up with creative ideas for her to help market her home-based business.

By the time I was in the ninth grade I had photographed my first wedding and found that I had a knack for photography. I began photographing friends and family and became quite good at it. Throughout high school and college I honed my photography skills and began freelancing for a photo studio part-time. After college I started my own photo business while I worked in local radio.

In a few years I quickly found that marketing was the key to this competitive industry. So I read everything that I could get my hands on, went to seminars, got a mentor, and quickly became very busy.

While doing some photo work for a client he offered me a job in advertising at a local independent television station. This intrigued me enough that I left the full-time photography business to go into the glitzy world of television advertising and marketing.

Even though I was 'sales person of the month' almost every month, it was not long until I saw that this was not glitzy or even lucrative working for a small indy.

However, I did learn a lot about local business marketing from calling on and working with a lot of small to medium sized business owners.

Since I did enjoy this business and thought I could get better at it I decided to take a leap of faith and move to a larger market. Again I became a sponge and soaked up as much knowledge as I possibly could.

Soon thereafter, at the age of 28, I had branded myself as a good sales manager candidate and was offered the position to manage a television station in my hometown of Savannah, Georgia.

I could tell you a lot of stories about these times, but the experience I gained and the education I received while in this position was worth more than a doctorate degree.

After just two short years, with the help of the new staff that was formed, we took our station to the number one spot in Adults 18-49 for this market. A feat that was unbelievable by most, especially our competition.

I have since worked many more years in this industry and in more markets working with more and more small to medium sized businesses and professionals, learning and gathering information, ideas, techniques and successes from each.

My career began to take more of an online focus in 2003 and now I work for **You** in personal branding and interactive marketing.

Over the last ten years or so, the internet has taken a new course of direction for business professionals. **Traditional media is changing** rapidly and interactive media is taking its place.

From online Display advertising to Video, Search Engine Marketing, Pay-Per-Click advertising, Affiliate Marketing, Email Marketing, Mobile Marketing, Social Media and more. Consumers have made the shift and are accepting it more every day.

Because of this shift, the old way of pushing out an advertising message is falling quickly. As consumers, we are way too busy, are very connected by mobile, and are bombarded by over 3,000 outbound marketing interruptions per day. Getting through the clutter has become almost impossible with traditional media.

This has made way for marketing thought leaders to discover the successes of Personal Branding and Marketing yourself rather than a company. Rather than do outbound marketing to the masses of people who are trying to block you out, I advocate "personal branded marketing" where you help yourself "get found" by people already searching for, learning about, and shopping in your industry.

In order to do this, you need a website, or blog, that is set up like a "hub" for your industry that attracts visitors naturally through the search engines, through the blogosphere, and through the social media sites.

I believe most marketers today spend 90% of their efforts on outbound marketing and 10% on personal branded marketing and I advocate that those ratios flip.

1

What Is Personal Branded Marketing?

Personal Branded Marketing is inbound marketing focused on getting you found by customers or potential customers.

In traditional marketing (outbound marketing) companies or salespeople focus on finding customers. They use techniques that are poorly targeted and that interrupt people. They use cold-calling, print advertising, radio advertising, junk mail, spam and trade shows.

Technology is making these techniques less effective and more expensive. Caller ID blocks cold calls, TiVo makes TV advertising less effective, spam filters block mass emails and tools like RSS are making print and Newspaper advertising less effective. It's still possible to get a message out via these channels, but it costs more.

Personal Branded Marketers flip outbound marketing on its head.

Instead of interrupting people with television ads, they create videos that potential customers want to see. Instead of buying newspaper and print ads, they create their own blog that people subscribe to and look forward to reading. Instead of cold calling, they create useful content and tools so that people call them looking for more information.

Instead of driving their message into a crowd over and over again like a sledgehammer, they attract highly qualified customers to their business like a magnet.

Think about this for a moment. As a professional, what if your clients or customers sought you out instead of you seeking them? What if you were able to set up a system that brought in a steady flow of new prospects for your product or service on a regular basis?

That's what happens when you brand yourself as a thought leader and an expert in your field.

When you need to have your car repaired, you take it to a mechanic. When you have a leaky toilet, you call in a plumber. When you need to sell your home, you contact your Realtor.

So why not position yourself as the go-to professional that your clients and prospects automatically call when they need your product or service?

You can do this with personal branding.

The most successful Personal Branded Marketing campaigns have three key components that help you **stand out from the crowd**:

(1) Content - Content is the substance of any Personal Branded Marketing campaign. It is the information or tool that attracts potential customers to your site or your business.

(2) Search Engine Optimization - SEO makes it easier for potential customers to find your content. It is the practice of building your site and inbound links to your site to maximize your ranking in search engines, where most of your customers begin their buying process.

(3) Social Media - Social media amplifies the impact of your content. When your content is distributed across and discussed on networks of personal relationships, it becomes more authentic and nuanced, and is more likely to draw qualified customers to you.

There are three specific ways Personal Branded "Inbound" Marketing improves on the efficiency of traditional marketing:

(1) It Costs Less

Outbound marketing means spending money - either by buying ads, buying email lists or renting huge booths at trade shows. Personal Branded Marketing is creating content and talking about it. A blog costs nothing to start. A Twitter account is free, too. Both can draw thousands of customers to you. The marketing ROI from inbound campaigns is higher. Let's say you sell advertising. If you have a blog where you consistently write articles that are relevant to your potential customers and they read your articles, you are branding and positioning yourself as an expert on advertising to your potential clients.

(2) Better Targeting

Techniques like cold-calling, mass mail and email campaigns are notoriously poorly targeted. You're reaching out to individuals because of one or two attributes in a database. When you do Personal Branded Marketing, you only approach people who self-qualify themselves.

They demonstrate an interest in your content, so they are likely to be interested in your product. Continuing as an advertising salesperson, your blog, or website, has a form that customers can complete to receive a FREE report to find out the top 10 best words to use in local advertising.

Now when your potential client completes the form to receive your free report, you capture their name and email so that you can continue to target them and market to them. We'll cover more on this a little later.

(3) It's an Investment, Not an Ongoing Expense

When you buy pay-per-click advertising on search engines,

its value is gone as soon as you pay for it. In order to maintain a position at the top of Google's paid results, you have to keep paying. However, if you invest that money in quality content that ranks in Google's organic results, you'll be there until somebody displaces you.

People are tired of traditional advertising. They are sick of "being sold" and want to make purchases in a completely different environment.

Research clearly suggests that consumers are moving *away* from trusting traditional advertising and moving *toward* trusting their friends, their networks and the networks that they have created around themselves.

More and more people are moving online to establish a network of trusted friends and colleagues. They are active in social networking sites, business networking sites, sharing sites, and publishing sites.

If you want to capture the attention of this new consumer behavior, then you will need to move online as well!

Even though there are literally *thousands of options*, there's no need to be overwhelmed because now you are going to learn how to use the top five to eight social networking sites that will work well for you.

Stay plugged in and I promise that this book will be an invaluable resource in assisting you in exploding your business like never before.

Keep in mind that your personal positioning will not happen overnight. It does take time. But if you keep with it, maintain your brand throughout all the platforms you are engaged in, and continue to grow your network, you will begin to see results.

I personally can tell you that I am contacted every week with potential new clients. Not all of them turn into business for me, but I am given the opportunity to at least make an attempt at converting someone into a new client.

Let's now get right into the meat of things…

2

Relationship Marketing

Think about it for a minute. Don't you prefer to do business with someone that you know and trust? This is basically what relationship marketing is all about.

Relationship marketing is about developing relationships with individuals *before* you show them your product or service.

This approach works amazingly well in today's market place! **People are much more willing to take action when they know and trust someone.**

I would suggest that you not blatantly advertise your services / business. Instead, using social media you are going to meet new people, build trust and then *offer them valuable, free advice over and over again.*

In today's world a person is not going to randomly fork over money to someone they do not know and trust. You are going to instead build a relationship with your potential customers first, then they will seek you out when they need your service or product.

So, how and where do you start to develop relationships with people? You go to *where potential clients are congregating by the millions! Not physically, but online!*

You become involved in some of the most popular Social Media websites in the world.

You want to do this strategically, though, and that is where this book comes in. I'm going to cover the most important websites for you to get involved in and how to get involved.

There are a ton of different categories of sites that exist and even more sub-categories within these sites. However, you've got to be strategic about which sites you want to be involved in because once you get involved you need to be active on the sites as well. Don't let that statement scare you away because you are going to learn how to spend as little or as much time as you want. You can actually maintain your social media sites with only 20 – 30 minutes per day.

Here are some of the different **categories** of sites that exist:

- Blogs
- Social Networks
- Article Directories
- Press Release Sites
- Video Sharing
- Podcasting
- Presentation sharing
- Meetups
- Social Bookmarking
- Photosharing
- Discussion Boards/Forums

Of course, there are lots more categories that can be found and even industry-specific categories that you should consider as well, but in this writing, I didn't want you to get too overwhelmed with loads and loads of information.

You will pick up more information as we progress through Personal Branded Marketing. If you stay plugged in you can become the expert in your field.

What I am going to do, instead of going through tons of platforms that you can use as part of your Personal Branded Marketing, I'm going to highlight some that I highly suggest that you participate in, while focusing specifically on five of them.

While these are not all the sites that I recommend, these are the top sites that I feel are the best in assisting with Personal Branded Marketing:

1) LinkedIn
2) Facebook
3) Twitter
4) YouTube
5) Biznik

Another reason that I highly recommend these particular five marketing platforms is that you are utilizing a full spectrum of marketing strategies.

All five of these marketing platforms have *unique characteristics*: LinkedIn is a business networking site, Facebook is a social networking site, Twitter is a social microblog, YouTube is an online video sharing site and Biznik is a business networking site specifically for small to medium sized business.

When you combine the power of *all five* of these marketing platforms, you deliver an **"impressive visibility"** campaign that places you and your business in front of as many potential customers as possible.

The elemental objective of your Personal Branded Marketing is to create authentic relationships with your potential customers so that they ultimately *visit your website or contact you.*

Even though this will not happen overnight, if you maintain an authoritative and dependable presence on your marketing platforms, your potential customers will notice and eventually react.

3

Social Media Marketing Rules of Engagement

There are a few ground rules that you need to be aware of before you start implementing your Social Media marketing.

I've often heard the analogy of social media being much like attending a cocktail party, in that you're going to get out as much as you are willing to put in.

You're going to meet people, chat, have some fun, and engage with them, but just like a cocktail party, it may take a little while before you get completely comfortable. Don't let this scare you off. Press forward and before you know it you will feel very capable and confident.

You're also going to meet people from all walks of life. There are going to be those that you will enjoy meeting and then there will be those that are a stick-in-the-mud! Just remember that this is YOUR marketing and you are in charge of who you want to become friends with and who you don't, who you choose to follow and who you choose to block.

Just as in all online endeavors, the one hard fast rule is **No Spamming!**

As long as you stay away from any sort of spam-like behavior, you aren't going to make "mistakes."

Don't forget to stop by and get to know me on all these platforms.

4

5 Key Elements to Personal Branded Marketing

1) Be Socialable

The main purpose that you are in these platforms is to build relationships with potential customers. The way to do this is to ask questions, answer questions, make comments and otherwise interact with your contacts. The whole purpose that you are here is to engage. If you don't engage with people, they are not going to engage with you.

2) Don't Address Rude People

There will most definitely be rude people that you will run across. I highly suggest that you just ignore them. Don't even acknowledge them. If you were to respond to a rude or negative person it will be right out in the open for everyone to see and is just not a good idea.

The best thing to do is just un-follow or block any difficult people. This will be done in the back-end of the platform, so nobody will have to see that you have done so. You should always keep your composure and be absolutely professional in all that you do.

(This is not the case if you are a company using social media as a customer service platform).

3) Keep Your Brand Consistent Throughout All Platforms

It's very important that you maintain consistency in your brand throughout all that you do. No matter which platform, you should keep your same profile information and photograph the same. This consistency will assist in creating trust with the people that you engage in these platforms. Remember, the more that someone trusts you and feels that they know you, the more likely they are to do business with you.

4) Do Not Blatantly Sell

We've talked about why not to sell and push out your message earlier. Potential customers will feel better about you if you DO NOT sell but rather provide information that they are looking for.

This will allow you to PULL in your customers once they find that you are providing them with what they are looking for. Let your website do your selling for you.

5) Be Prepared

As you engage in Personal Branded Marketing, attentive prospects will look for more information about you and your business. You have to offer them an easy, nonthreatening invitation to visit your website. When they come to your website, prospects should be able to access additional information, free advice, reports, and/or e-books in order to learn more about you.

The rest of this book will assist you in giving you a **simple, step-by-step guide on effectively using Social Media Platforms** to effectively market your business.

5

LinkedIn is a social networking site used by business professionals. The purpose of the site is to allow its users to keep a base of contact details of other business professionals. These people are referred to as *Connections*.

These connections can then be used in several ways:
Your network is constructed of your direct connections, the connections of each of their connections (second degree connections) and the connections of second degree connections (third degree connections).

Your connections can be used to acquire an introduction to someone you want to make contact with through a mutual trusted contact.

Your connections can also be used to find jobs, to network, and to create potential business partners endorsed by other connections within in your network.

You can also announce jobs and look for potential candidates.

Making connections with as many people as you can seems to be a mindset that many people in this platform seem to have. I believe it is more important to connect and reach out to people that you know and those that can and will benefit you in your business.

For example, you should not just begin sending invitations to connect with every single person that you can. Reach out to people that you feel like you have some sort of relationship with and invite them to connect with you.

Now you may receive invitations from all sorts of people from all walks of life from all over the world. I don't see a problem of accepting those invitations because you never know when someone you would like to be connected with may be connected to someone that reaches out to you and then you can ask for a introduction.

If all of this sounds a little confusing right now, just hang on. It gets easier to understand as we move forward.

6

Creating Your LinkedIn Profile

Log onto: http://www.LinkedIn.com to create your account.

1) Write your bio in "first person" (use "I") to make your profile read as a professional resume.

2) VERY IMPORTANT! Use a sharp and professional looking photo of yourself. It is extremely important that anyone viewing your profile can see that you are a real person representing your business.

3) Be sure that your bio includes as much professional information as possible including your education, previous job experiences, recognitions, relevant groups, and any other pertinent information about you or your business.

4) Then, make sure to add me as a "Connection" on LinkedIn not only see how I composed my bio, but I also would appreciate having you as a part of my network:
www.linkedin.com/in/leonespencer

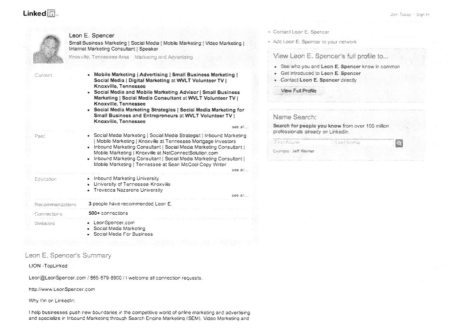

Here's a screenshot of my personal LinkedIn profile page.

As you can see, I'm using a professional image as my profile picture, (I use the same image in every platform) I have my profile fully completed, and I use Keywords that I want to be found for and known for in my title description.

It is important to use keywords in your 'specialties' section as well as all your past job titles. This will help you with your ranking inside of LinkedIn profiles. Your ranking is the order in which you will be listed with everyone else in your specific category or industry. More on this a little later on.

You can search for individuals in LinkedIn's people search and find out how your profile ranks within all other profiles within your specific business category.

For example, I want to be found in 'marketing' because that is my field of expertise. I also want to be found in 'small business marketing', 'mobile marketing', 'social media training', and several other areas so I constructed my profile using those keywords.

Now go login to LinkedIn.com and type 'small business marketing' into the people search. You will see that I show up fairly high in this search. You can also search the other keywords I mentioned above and I still should rank pretty high.

You too can get your profile ranked high. In fact, you can even rank higher than my profile if you write it correctly.

This is what I like to call Social Profile Optimization. Just as a website uses Search Engine Optimization, your profile can be written to rank you higher in some social media sites.

LinkedIn can help you tremendously with personal branding. As you rank your profile higher within the searches, people will find you in these searches and that helps position you as an expert within your field, or within your keywords.

Everyday, people are looking for someone in a specific field to help them solve a problem. If your profile is high up on the list of people within your field of expertise, then you have a better chance of someone finding and contacting you when they need your product or service.

This is especially helpful when you are looking for a job. If you rank high in your field it makes it easy for recruiters to find you and it also shows them that you stand out in your industry.

7

How To Market On LinkedIn

Here are some tips to assist you in marketing **more effectively on** LinkedIn:

1) Market Through The Use of Your Profile

Make sure to complete your profile to 100%. Make sure to use a sharp, professional photo and as much professional information about yourself as possible.

Bear in mind, that LinkedIn is a networking site for professionals, so you want to emphasize this part of your business to potential prospects.

Your profile will be seen many times as you make connections. It also can very likely get found in Search Engines when people type in a search for your name (or even your company). So, be sure that your profile is the best that it can be and that it includes how people can contact you and why they should contact you!

2) Build Your Network by Adding Connections

This can be somewhat of a timely process. LinkedIn also has a strict policy that you are only supposed to ask people that you *personally know* to become a connection. So, first of all you want to search for any of your connections through business, school, organizations, church, past employment, etc. Customize a note asking if they will join your LinkedIn network.

Then, join the LinkedIn Group *TopLinked*. This group is comprised of people who consider themselves **Open Networkers**. They generally connect with *most* everyone who asks. Once you are a member of this group you can send fellow group members an invitation to connect. In fact you should join other appropriate groups where you will also be able to make connections. Always include a personal note when you send an invitation.

It could be something like this: *"Hi Ricky! I noticed that we are both group members of **Mobile Marketing for small business**. I thought I'd reach out to you and see if we could connect here on LinkedIn. I'd like to have you as part of my network. Thanks, Leon Spencer"*

3) Ask For Recommendations

Recommendations are a significant part of the LinkedIn network. There are some people who have over a hundred recommendations. You should shoot to have at minimum 5-10.

You cannot ask someone you do not know for a recommendation, so be strategic about who you do ask. You can, however, ask a former colleague or business associate, or a client and even someone you work with now to write you a short recommendation that you can use on LinkedIn. It does not need to be more than a paragraph.

4) Get Engaged in the LinkedIn Forums

This is a great way to start making connections with other LinkedIn Members. In LinkedIn you have the ability to ask any question pertaining to business. If you have a marketing question, all you need to do is ask.

Once you post your question, there will be a lot of people that will respond. As these people do respond, you can always ask them to consider becoming your connection as well.

5) *Answer questions* within the LinkedIn Forums

Just as you ask questions, you should also answer them. This will assist you in positioning yourself as an expert. You should login on a regular basis and drill down into your specific category of business and find the questions that are being asked.

You will notice that as you begin answering questions, others will perceive you as an expert in your particular industry. You will bring more exposure to yourself and to your business as you answer others' questions.

If you login to the questions section where your potential clients may be located and begin to answer questions there, then this will further brand you as an expert within your business category.

6) Join Groups Associated With Your Business or Your Prospect's Business

Find groups that are associated with your business and join them. Then begin engaging with the members in these groups. Of course, as you begin interacting with the different group members you will soon find that some will become connections for your business network.

Once you are a member of a group, you can send them a personal invitation to connect with you.

It is my opinion that it is far more important to join groups where your potential customers may be located and when you become active in those groups and forums, it will only further your positioning as the expert within your industry. For example, if you sell to automobile dealers, then you should join the groups for automobile dealers. If you sell to Realtors, join the groups where Realtors are members.

7) Create Your Own Group and Announce It To Your Network

One of the best ways to position yourself as an expert is to create your own LinkedIn group and invite your connections to join.

As the leader of a LinkedIn group, you will have a tremendous amount of credibility. By creating a valuable group and offering great content and information to your members, you will build a great following!

Keep in mind, though, that if you are going to build a group, you need to commit to being there on a regular basis and provide content to the group on a regular basis.

As you can see, there are several ways to begin your marketing on LinkedIn. Make sure to follow the rules, avoid blatant advertising and offer great content. It won't take long to build a huge network of professional connections.

8) List Your Events or Webinars in the Events Section

Under the 'more' tab there is a section called 'events'. You can list any sort of event that you believe will help you reach out to your potential clients in this section. List here if you are holding a webinar, or a customer appreciation event, etc. Any opportunity that you might have that wherein you can make contact with your potential clients or customers can be listed here.

When listing your event, make sure to use keywords in your event title and description as Google can index this page giving you additional online exposure.

For more on using **LinkedIn** as a marketing tool, visit: www.LeonSpencer.com
The site is filled with great articles, tips, techniques, and ideas to assist you in making LinkedIn work for you and your business.

8

Facebook is the one of the largest social networking sites in the world based on the idea of connecting and reconnecting with "friends" who share common interests, goals, etc.

As a member of the Facebook community, you create a profile and then invite your friends into your network.

Once your friends join your network they are able to view your photos, videos, web pages, marketing pages and groups.

Friends are also able to send email to one another, write on each other's "walls" send announcements, etc.

As a professional, or as a business, you can create profiles, or pages, other than your personal page. This is where you will build your personal brand as a professional within your field of expertise. You will be able to upload attractive graphics or images of yourself or brand or logo or whatever you choose to use.

There are also a lot of ways to use this Facebook page to assist you in building a list of potential prospects for your product or service.

The latest Facebook design, as of this writing, will allow you to install HTML code on your Facebook pages. So, essentially you can create a mini-website within Facebook complete with links to other web pages or sites or even your blog.

Some examples of how to create your Facebook page will follow.

9

Create Your FaceBook Profile and Account

Log onto: http://www.Facebook.com and create your account.

1) Write your bio in "first person" (use "I") to make your profile read as a professional resume.

2) VERY IMPORTANT! Use a sharp and professional looking photo of yourself. It is extremely important that anyone viewing your profile can see that you are a real person representing your business.

3) Add professional information to the *profile box under your photo* and include links to your websites.

4) Depending on whether you are using this for professional purposes or personal purposes, you will include as much personal information as possible using the "edit my profile" button under your photo.

If you are using Facebook for professional purposes, people will still want to know the personal side of you, but just be aware of what you are putting out there for people to know and see.

You can include your favorite movies, interests, quotes, books, etc. This will help other users get to know you on a more individual level.

5) Then, make sure to "Become a Fan" of mine on Facebook so that you can take a look at my Facebook Profile:
http://fb.leonspencer.com

Here's a screenshot of my Facebook Fan Page. As you can see, I've utilized the left column with a graphic that represents my personal branding. I also have my blog linked to my page so that when I write a blog post it will automatically post on my Facebook page.

I don't think that it's as important to have a ton of friends in social media as it is to be connected to people that count in building your personal brand.

Depending on exactly what you want to use your Facebook page for, you can use a personal page or you can create a Fan page, or both.

With as many people that are in Facebook, it makes a great tool in building your personal brand. Just as in your blog, your content is what will make people connect with you in Facebook. Post relevant content and your Facebook following will grow.

The more it grows, the more people you can influence with your message and your brand. This goes for a large company as well as an individual.

10

How To Market On Facebook

Here are a some tips to help you market more effectively on FaceBook:

1) Market Through The Use of Your Profile

Make sure that your profile is 100% complete and that it's interesting. Never post photos that are unprofessional or would cause questions of your image or character with potential customers. Always use a sharp, professional headshot.

Your profile will be seen many times as you make friends. It also can very likely get found in Search Engines when people type in a search for your name (or even your company). So, be sure that your profile is the best that it can be and that it includes how people can contact you and why they should contact you!

In fact, if your profile is well done, many people will comment on it and even ask your advice on certain subjects. Do not make the mistake of having a poor-quality profile that offers little value to your visitors.

2) Send Friend Requests

One objective for you here on Facebook, is to make connections with potential clients and customers who may eventually need your products or services.

Find groups that are associated with your business and join them. Then begin engaging with the members in these groups. Of course, as you begin interacting with the different group members you will soon find that some will become friends and fans of your business.

It's also wise to join groups where your potential customers may be congregating and when you become active in those groups and forums, it will only further your positioning as the expert within your industry.

Begin making friend requests to specific individuals who are involved in the groups. When you make a friend request, you should always add a personal note to your request.

It could be like this: *"Hi! I noticed that we are both group members of **Inbound Marketing**. I thought I'd reach out to you and see if we could become friends here on Facebook. I'd love for you to "Become a Fan".* http://fb.leonspencer.com
Thanks, Leon Spencer"

Facebook allows you to request up to fourty friends per day, so follow their rules.

3) Update Your Status Several Times EVERYDAY

All Facebook users are able to "update their status" as often as they would like. Every time you update your status, you have a personal Facebook "newsfeed" that broadcasts your update to all of your Facebook friends.

My advice is to change up your status updates with professional content (blog posts, twitter posts, articles, etc) and appropriate personal information. And, of course, stay away from blatant advertising!

4) Host An Event And Post It

As your Facebook Fan-base builds, you should consider hosting an event. It doesn't have to be a LIVE event. It can be as simple as a webinar or teleseminar.

For example, if you are a marketing professional, you can host a free webinar where people can "Learn how to leverage social media networking for business".

Post your event to your profile and invite your customers who could be your Fans/Friends to attend.

5) Share Videos

Whenever you post a new video or picture, your "newsfeed" will automatically distribute these to all of your fans/friends.

When you create video for your YouTube Channel, *(this is another tool that I will teach you to use at: LocalBrandedU.com),* post a link to the video on your Facebook page. This will assist you with your continued efforts of building your brand and image as an expert in your industry.

6) Engage With Your Fans/Friends - Write on Their Walls Or Comment On Their Status Updates

Another objective you want to accomplish is to develop relationships with your fans/friends. Therefore, you'll need to take time once in a while to visit some of your fans/friends profile pages and write messages on their walls. You can also scan the updates that your fans/friends make from your Homepage. You can make quick comments on their status updates in just a short amount of time.

Make sure that your are not blatantly advertising, all you want to do is simply make comments, ask questions or wish them a good day.

7) Create a Facebook Group

All Facebook users can create groups that others can join. Facebook groups are where people to come together to share opinions and interests about a unique subject.

For example, if you own a photography lab, you can create a "Photographer's Digital Tips Group" and invite your Facebook friends to become a part of your group.

As the administrator of the group, your name and information is public knowledge. In addition, group administrators are able to email their members with information about the group. But, Facebook groups do not have newsfeeds or status updates. Group members must log into the group to participate.

8) Create a Facebook Fan Page

A professional, or business can create a Facebook Fan Page to promote their business, interact with fans and assist in establishing a stronger brand identity.

Your personal FaceBook page is your own **personal profile**. You are only allowed one profile and a maximum of 5,000 friends.

Your business page, or Fan Page, can have an unlimited number of friends, or 'LIKES'.

Like your personal profile, you can build a Fan Page for your business and it can be optimized with rich media and interactive applications. You can use your Facebook Fan Page as a lead capture page, an informational page, a promotional page and more. It can basically be a mini-website.

In addition, as you update your status, add links and post videos, and your fans will be notified in their newsfeed. Therefore, Fan Pages are a lot like Personal Profiles. It is important that you strategically use your Fan Page to publish high quality content to your fans and NO Blatant Advertising!

As I mentioned a little earlier, the new Facebook design

Be creative! Use a custom background that will keep your image and brand consistent throughout all of your social media platforms. The **BEST** place to get a custom background is: http://Facebook.com/FanDevelopment

Of course, become my Fan so that you don't miss out on any marketing tips, ideas, techniques and strategies!

To create your own **FaceBook Fan Page**, login to
http://www.facebook.com/pages/create.php.

The page looks like this and you can choose which type of Fan page you want to create.

Facebook is a very powerful place to market yourself and your business.

For more on using **Facebook** as a marketing tool, visit:
www.LeonSpencer.com
The site is filled with great articles, tips, techniques, and ideas to assist you in making Facebook work for you and your business.

11

Twitter is a free social networking and micro-blogging service that lets users send and read other users' updates (or tweets) which are text-based posts of up to 140 characters in length.

Updates are shown on the user's profile page and delivered to other users who have signed up to receive them.

According to Twitter.com: *Twitter is a free service that lets you keep in touch with people through the exchange of quick, frequent answers to one simple question: What are you doing?*

Just as in other social media networks, Twitter can be used for personal branding as well. There are several ways that you can do this and I will touch on a few in this chapter.

The best way to become familiar with the platform is to get in and begin listening, or watching what is going on. It can be a little over-whelming when you first get started because of the speed and amount of messages going through the system. But after you understand how it works, you'll feel more comfortable.

Twitter has been instrumental in not only assisting professionals with personal branding, but has even been credited for assisting in the fall of governments in the Middle-East to minute-by-minute updates of trials.

As a marketing tool, Twitter has many uses. One, of course, is connecting with your potential prospects or clients, and keeping them informed about you and your products or services.

You can do this in real time, so if you have a new product launch or if you are at a tradeshow or convention, you can keep your followers updated instantly as to any information you want to send out.

Just as in all your social media platforms, make sure that your content is relevant to your followers, otherwise they will not stay connected.

12

Create Your Twitter Account And Profile

Log onto: http://www.Twitter.com and create your account.

1) Write your profile in the "first person" (use"I").

2) VERY IMPORTANT! Use a sharp and professional looking photo of yourself. It is extremely important that anyone viewing your profile can see that you are a real person representing your business.

3) I strongly suggest that you **DO NOT** use the Twitter default background. Be creative! Use a different background that you can find for free online or have a professional background produced that will keep your image and brand consistent throughout all of your social media platforms. The **<u>BEST</u>** place to get a custom background is: http://SocialBrandedMedia.com

4) Include the URL to your business website or Blog.

5) Tell what you do in short terms and be bold and to the point. Be professional and friendly.

Make sure to follow me on Twitter:
http://www.twitter.com/LeonESpencer

Here's a screenshot of my Twitter profile page. As you can see, I'm not using the default background, but instead I've had a custom background created that promotes my personal brand and my field of work.

You too should use a custom Twitter background instead of the default background. You can get a custom background produced very inexpensively. Usually for less than $100. There are also a lot of sites where you can get a free twitter background that you can make your own.

Use your background to promote your brand with all your contact information that you want to be found. You should promote your website or blog, and list any other pertinent information that will help you in building your brand.

If you use an image of yourself, make sure to use the same image that you are using in all your other social media profiles.

13

FIVE Ways To Post On Twitter

1) General Post (Tweet)

You can type a message in your Twitter account, click **"update"** and it will become available to all the people who are following you.
Example: Working on a great Social Media Campaign. Can't wait to share it!

2) Twitter Reply

You are also able to talk or reply to *specific* Twitter users. You type **@ and then their user name directly after that**. When someone replies to you or your message, you will see your user name with the symbol @ before it.
*Example: **Hey** @leonespencer! That was a great article on Social Media ROI.*

3) Twitter RT

If you like a post that was made, you can **"Retweet"** the post. You simply **type RT@ followed by their user name, followed by the entire post.**
Example: RT @leonespencer The Untimate Expression of Belief is Action – Anthony Milan

4) Twitter DM

If you want to send a **private message** to one of your followers, you can send them a **direct message**. Type the letters **dm with the person's user name**. You receive private messages from others on a separate page of Twitter.

Example: dm leonespencer Please let me know the day and time of your next webinar. Thanks!

5) Twitter Hashtag

Twitter has **specific categories or hot topics** that
people are Tweeting about. If you want to join in that particular conversation, you type **# followed by the topic** as a signal that you are referring to that particular topic in your Twitter post.

Example: You will benefit greatly from following @leonespencer #FollowFriday

14

How To Market On Twitter

Here are some tips to help you use Twitter as a dynamic marketing tool:

1) Market Through The Use of Your Profile

Twitter is not like any other social networking sites in that your profile is only a few short words. This can also be used to your advantage because you have the opportunity of your entire profile being seen and read! You have to make sure to use your words very succinctly.   Just as a powerful headline describes a great article, so should your profile on Twitter.

Allow your potential followers to know who you are through your profile description. In my case my Twitter profile reads: **Marketing Specialist | Advertising and Interactive Media Strategist | Mobile Marketer | Speaker | Author | Social Media Marketer | Boxer Dog Parent.** Remember that this short description will most likely be the decision on whether someone follows you or not!

2) Your Content (TWEETS) Have Got To Be Valuable

Make sure that you **never blatantly advertise your product or service** on Twitter. This would be a HUGE MISTAKE!

You can however, put links to helpful blog posts or articles that you have written. Don't get stuck *only posting links* to your own material. The 80/20 rule should be your guide.   Post links to your own material 20% of the time; engage, interact and converse 80% of the time. The reason you are on Twitter is to create relationships. The only way to do this is by joining in on the conversations.

3) Interact

Twitter is actually a social networking tool. Therefore, if you are going to benefit from it, then you've got to use it as it was meant to be used! It was not designed as a way to generate self-promotion or for one-sided conversations. To be in the Twitter elite, you simply need to become involved. The number one reason Twitter won't work for you is that you are *not interacting enough with your followers.*

4) Ask Questions

Ask your followers or those you are following **questions**. Your questions do not have to be thought-provoking all the time. They don't even have to be business related all the time. The key to Twitter is to engage!

5) Answer Questions

If you have a follower that asks a question that you know the answer to, be sure to answer it. You will get a lot out of this platform if you use it. People will engage with you and come to appreciate your value to them very quickly! Answering questions that are related to your particular specialty is a great way to establish yourself as an expert.

6) Keep It Fun!

Since you can only use 140 characters on Twitter, keep things light and fun.

Remember, that it's as easy to "unfollow" as it is to "follow" you. Twitter can be a very commanding tool *if used properly*. By utilizing these Twitter tips, you will begin to grow a large following on Twitter.

For more on using **Twitter** as a marketing tool, visit: www.LeonSpencer.com

The site is filled with great articles, tips, techniques, and ideas to assist you in making Twitter work for you and your business.

15

YouTube is a video sharing site where users can upload, view, and share video clips.

Unregistered users can watch most of the videos, while registered users are permitted to upload an unlimited number of videos.

YouTube has made it possible for anyone with access to a computer to post a video that millions of people can watch within a few minutes. The wide range of topics covered by YouTube has turned video sharing into one of the most important parts of the internet culture.

Video is the hottest thing on the internet today! In fact, in my opinion, it's the reason why Google purchased YouTube. They recognized the trends in internet video, and seized an opportunity.

If you think about it, when you visit a website you have come to expect there to be video on the site.

As a professional wanting to build a personal brand, there is no better way to do it than by using video.

YouTube is the number one video site online. The number two video site is YouTube Mobile. In this chapter, I'm going to tell you ways that you can use YouTube to capitalize on building your personal brand.

So, as you are reading this chapter, be thinking of some particular videos that you can create that not only will assist you in telling people who you are, but also what you do and why they should do business with you.

16

Create Your YouTube Profile and Account

Log onto: http://www.YouTube.com and create your account.

1) Write your profile in the "first person" (use"I").

2) VERY IMPORTANT! Use a sharp and professional looking photo of yourself. It is extremely important that anyone viewing your profile can see that you are a real person representing your business.

3) I strongly suggest that you **DO NOT** use the YouTube default background. Be creative! Use a different background that you can have professionally produced that will keep your image and brand consistent throughout all of your social media platforms. The **BEST** place to get a custom background is: http://SocialBrandedMedia.com

4) Include a link to your website at the TOP of your profile and at the bottom of your profile.

5) Make sure to 'friend' me and **subscribe to my YouTube channel:** http://www.youtube.com/leonespencer

Here's a screenshot of my YouTube channel. You should continue with your personal brand with your YouTube channel as well. You can find a design that will transfer to all your profiles very easily.

You can even create a video for your channel that will introduce you and what you do. You can then set this video to be your opening video everytime someone visits your channel.

Video is the hottest thing on the internet. I highly suggest that you create videos and create them often. There's even services you can use to email your videos to your followers once you have them created.

17

How To Market On YouTube

Video marketing is probably *THE* most powerful way to **attract new business** and new customers.

One reason that video marketing is so effective is that your potential clients and customers can get to know you. Immediately you will begin building trust with your viewer when they see, hear and watch how you present what you are saying.

Here are a few points to keep in mind when using YouTube to market your business:

1) Offer something of value in your videos

Never blatantly advertise or promote your business. You should always produce videos that will provide quality content and information that your potential clients or customers are searching for.

If you are a business coach then give tips and ideas that you know your potential clients are looking for. If you are a Realtor, then offer up the "Top 10 Factors to consider while inspecting a potential new home." If you always offer value, you will build a huge following fast.

2) Have Fun

Because of the culture of YouTube, it's the perfect place to have some fun.
You can crack jokes, laugh, smile and be humorous. Just keep in mind what your purpose of the video is and don't stray off topic. I guess what I'm trying to say is make it light-hearted…it will go a long way!

3) Keep It Professional

Of course you are not a Hollywood producer. But, on the same token, keep your video as professional as possible. Dress appropriately, make sure your surroundings are not distracting, and keep it simple. View some of your competitors on YouTube to see what they are doing, then do it better!

You only have a few seconds at the beginning of the video to come across as a professional that knows what you are talking about. Make good use of this time.

4) Use Good Lighting and Audio

You might as well not even produce a video if you don't have good lighting and sound. Before you upload your videos double check that the lighting and sound are at good levels. If you don't have the money to buy a nice light, just use available window light. It will look natural and should work fine.

Make sure to **speak loud enough and clear enough** that your viewers will understand you without any problems.

5) Use Target Key Words In Your Title and Tags

As you describe your video on your page, take some time to think about a great title and description. Your Title and Description will act as your SEO (Search Engine Optimization) when users are searching for your content.

In addition, you will want to add "tags" (keywords) that will help your video get found. The Realtor could use tags such as: *how to visually inspect a roof, Home Inspection tips, How to Buy a Home.*

6) Comment On Other Videos

Take the time to find popular YouTube videos related to your industry and post comments. This will give you additional exposure and may even bring people over to your own YouTube channel for a visit.

YouTube is an awesome platform for marketing your business and if you use it effectively, it will help you to EXPLODE your business!

Equipment

I'm not going to spend much time on equipment because everyone has their own opinions on what to use to create your videos, but I do have a couple of VERY important suggestions.

I would highly suggest that you invest in a video camera that will allow you the ease of uploading your video to your computer. You can get a video camera for very little. They start as low as $100 and go up from there. But most importantly, get a video camera that has an external microphone plug-in. A video is basically useless if the audio is bad. Take the time to find a video camera where you can plug an external mic into it and then get a nice microphone.

Microphones can be purchased for as little as $40 or so. If you are going to do this...do it right!

Make sure that when you shoot your video that you have adequate lighting and test, test, test.

For more on using **YouTube** as a marketing tool, visit: www.LeonSpencer.com
The site is filled with great articles, tips, techniques, and ideas to assist you in making YouTube work for you and your business.

18

Biznik is a community of entrepreneurs and small businesses dedicated to helping each other succeed.

Unlike LinkedIn, Biznik is for people who are building real businesses, not looking for their next job. It's for sharing your ideas, not posting your resume. It's the place where real conversations about small business and entrepreneurship are taking place.

Biznik is online AND face to face. Social networks are great. But nothing beats the power of a face-to-face meeting to build real, lasting business relationships and Biznik also promotes LIVE events.

Users maintain a "Network" of contacts. This network can then be used in several ways:

Your network is constructed of your direct connections through invitation.

Your network connections can be used to acquire an introduction to someone you want to make contact with through a mutual trusted contact.

Biznik is not as well-known as many of the other social networking platforms, but it is a very powerful platform when it comes to helping you build your personal brand.

When you build your profile in Biznik, you will not only be able to connect with others that you want to reach out to, but you will be able to use the platform to promote your products or services to a vast group of other professionals.

The power of this platform, in my opinion, is its strength in the search engines. Your profile will become highly visible on search engines like Google, Yahoo, and Bing.

This just makes it easier for potential clients or customers to find you.

19

Creating Your Biznik Profile

Log onto: http://www.Biznik.com to create your account.

1) Write your bio in "first person" (use "I") to make your profile read as a professional resume.

2) VERY IMPORTANT! Use a sharp and professional looking photo of yourself. It is extremely important that anyone viewing your profile can see that you are a real person representing your business.

3) Be sure that your bio includes as much professional information as possible including your education, previous job experiences, recognitions, relevant groups, and any other pertinent information about you or your business.

4) Then, make sure to invite me to your network. Look at how I composed my bio, get ideas from the wording etc. I would appreciate having you as a part of my network:
www.biznik.com/members/leon-spencer

Here's a screenshot of my Biznik profile page. Biznik is unique in that you can openly promote your business.

Most platforms do not allow you to outright promote your business, but the whole idea behind Biznik is to help the small business owner and the solopreneur and give them a platform to promote.

Use it wisely. Write articles and post often. You can even create your own group.

When you write an article for your blog, take it over to your Biznik profile and post it there as well. You can submit your articles so that they will show up as a featured article within the entire Biznik site if approved. This is a great way for you to not only get published but to stand out amongst all of the others in Biznik. Your article also has the chance of being indexed by the search engines giving you another opportunity of being found online by your potential clients and customers.

20

How To Market On Biznik

Here are some tips to assist you in marketing **more effectively on** Biznik:

1) Market Through The Use of Your Profile

Make sure to complete your profile is 100% complete. Make sure to use a sharp, professional photo and as much professional information about yourself as possible.

Keep in mind, that Biznik is a networking site for people in business, so you want to emphasize your business in your profile to potential prospects.

Your profile will be seen many times as you make connections. It also can very likely get found in Search Engines when people type in a search for your name, your category of business, or even your company. So, be sure that your profile is the best that it can be and that it includes how people can contact you and why they should contact you!

2) Build Your Network by Adding Connections

This can be somewhat of a timely process. Biznik has a great open policy on contacting others that you would like to have in your network.

Be professional! Don't SPAM anyone and remember that it's not a contest to see how many people you can get in your network. Keep in mind the real reason that you are building a network. It's to assist you in growing your business.

Do a search for other business people in your city or region and reach out to them first. Customize a note asking if they will join your Biznik network.

You should join appropriate groups where you will also be able to make connections. Always include a personal note when you send an invitation.

It could be something like this: *"Hi! I noticed that we are both group members of* **_Inbound Marketing_**. *I thought I'd reach out to you and see if we could connect here on Biznik. I'd love to have you as part of my network. Thanks, Leon Spencer"*

3) Get Engaged on Biz Talk Forums

This is a great way to start making connections with other Members. In Biznik you have the ability to ask any questions pertaining to your business needs. If you have a marketing question, all you need to do is ask.

Once you post your question, you there will be a lot of people that will respond. As these people do respond, you can always ask them to consider becoming your connection as well.

4) *Answer questions* within the Biz Talk Forums

Just as you ask questions, you should also answer them. This will assist you in positioning yourself as an expert.

You will notice that as you begin answering questions, others will perceive you as an expert in your particular industry. You will bring more exposure to yourself and to your business as you answer others' questions.

5) Join Groups Associated With Your Business or Your Prospect's Business

Find groups that are associated with your business and join them. Then begin engaging with the members in these groups. Of course, as you begin interacting with the different group members you will soon find that some will become connections for your business network.

It's also wise to join groups where your potential customers may be congregating and when you become active in those groups and forums, it will only further your positioning as the expert within your industry.

6) Create Your Own Group and Announce It To Your Network

One of the best ways to position yourself as an expert is to create your own Biznik group and invite your connections to join. As the leader of a Biznik group, you will have a tremendous amount of credibility. By creating a valuable group and offering great content and information to your members, you will build a great following!

As you can see, there are several ways to begin your marketing on Biznik. Make sure to follow the rules, avoid blatant advertising and offer great content. It won't take long to build a huge network of professional connections.

For more on using **Biznik** as a marketing tool, visit: www.LeonSpencer.com
The site is filled with great articles, tips, techniques, and ideas to assist you in making Biznik work for you and your business.

21

Pulling Your Personal Branded Marketing Plan Together

Now that you've got all of your accounts and profiles set-up, you're ready to begin energetically engaging in your social marketing platforms.

A common theme for those new to Personal Branded Marketing or Social Media Marketing is managing their time with these platforms. Many feel that Social Media Marketing is too overwhelming and takes way too much of their time.

Those that are new to this are not quite sure what to focus their time and energy on and what sometimes happens is they end up spending hours with the platforms and getting frustrated and eventually leaving.

It does not have to take that long. It does take time, but there are ways that you can automate some of that and there are ways that you can also outsource it very inexpensively. This all depends on the level of participation that you want to put towards your marketing.

For example, if you have a blog that you post on, you can set it to automatically post to your LinkedIn page or to your Facebook page fairly easily. There are applications within the platforms that make this an easy process to implement. Just do a search within the platforms for 'How to import Blog' and you will get what you need.

This will be a great time saving element for you when you are wanting to post information across several platforms.

Be consistent

One good piece of advice is to be consistent throughout every platform that you are in. If you are posting as a professional sales person in one platform, make sure that you are doing that in the others. Don't post personal content in one and business in another. Be consistent.

However, you still want to let your connections know that you are a real person. So, a good rule of thumb is to post business information 80 percent of the time and post more casual personal type information 20 percent of the time. Another way to look at this is to only be 'selling' your product or service 20 percent of the time and use the other 80 percent to post relevant information that helps your connections or followers with their own issues or business problems.

One BIG key to success is to giveaway as much value for free as you can. If you have tips, techniques, or ideas that you think will help your followers and connections, make sure to let them know. Give it to them often.

Relevant value is an important key to attracting a lot of attention to yourself online.

22

5 Time-Management Strategies For The Local Branded Marketer

1) Focus

There are **hundreds of platforms** to choose from and there's no way that you can be in all of them. You need to choose 5-8 and focus on those platforms. You cannot dominate your category if you spread yourself too thin. Pick the platforms that make the most sense for your business and focus solely on those.

2) Set Specific Time Each Day

Every day you will need to update and keep fresh the content in your social media platforms. Set aside time for development and maintenance.

Shoot a quick video, write a short article, update status in Facebook or LinkedIn. This doesn't have to be a long drawn out process. Just focus on what you need to do and get the tasks done. You can shoot a short video for your YouTube Channel and get it uploaded all within about 15 minutes. A blog post only needs to be a couple of paragraphs about something of value for your customers.

If you divide your time between developing information and maintenance, you will be working smarter.

3) Set An Allotted Amount Of Time For Marketing Each Day

Approach your marketing with a plan and work your plan every day. Part of your plan should be how much time you focus on marketing your business. To simply just start working on marketing is like throwing a dart at a dart board that you can't even see. You've got to put your plan in writing and follow the plan as best as you can. In running a business there's always going to be little things that steal your time, but if you focus, you will still find a way to get it done.

And like I said earlier, if you are at the point where you know that you need to be doing these things and focusing on your Personal Marketing, Social Media, and your website, and you truly do not have the time, there are companies that specialize in this and you can outsource it. There are many great companies that offer this service. Find someone that you like and trust and to steal a phrase from Nike, Just Do It!

4) Automate Your Accounts

Take the time to connect your social media and information accounts that you can connect.

For example, you can add your Twitter account to your Facebook account.
Then, whenever you update your status on one, it will automatically update the other.

Again, you can add your Blog to your FaceBook account, so that your Blog posts appear on your FaceBook page. Automating accounts will save you a ton of time and keep your brand consistent as well.

5) Recycle Your Efforts

Whenever you write an article, plan to reuse it in other platforms. Here is an
example: If you wrote an article entitled, "5 Ways To Become an Expert in Your Industry." You would, of course, publish that article to your blog.

However, it doesn't stop there. You could subsequently post that same article to your Facebook page and even send out a Tweet about the post. Then you could produce a short video about the same content for YouTube, and you could take the article and read it to produce a Podcast.

So you see, there are always multiple uses from your efforts. You don't have to create tons of content every day. Use your content wisely and in multiple locations and you will be effectively managing both your time and energy.

23

What do I do from here?

You've learned how marketing has changed and why **Personal Branded Marketing** is today's best way to advertise and market yourself or a local business.

If you are a local business owner, you can not only create a huge following of customers, but you will set yourself apart from all of your competitors and you will be able to build your personal brand as the expert within your local market.

In addition, you have learned the basics of creating accounts and profiles on five Social Networking and Marketing sites.

This book just gets you going and only covers the fundamentals of understanding all of the concepts behind your **Personal Branded Marketing.**

However, when you are ready to take it to the next level (the six and seven-figure a year level!), make sure to visit: www.LocalBrandedU.com

The **Local Branded University program** will give you instant access to hundreds of tips, strategies and techniques for EXPLODING your local business using primarily free and very LOW-COST marketing tools.

This website can be your lifeline to ongoing learning and assist you in building a huge following of prospects and clients. You will gain more in-depth knowledge on how to best utilize each of the social media platforms discussed here in this book as well as others.

You will find articles and videos that will guide you through the best ways to use the platforms for your personal branding.

Now is the time to implement a **Personal Branded Marketing** plan and grow your business like never before!

So, don't wait any longer. I'm ready to help you every step of the way!

You can find articles and more on my personal website: www.LeonSpencer.com

and

If I can ever be of any assistance to you or your company, feel free to contact me:

Leon Spencer
leon@leonspencer.com

24

Bonus Chapter

Your Main Street Marketing 3.0 Action Plan

Now that you know how social media can play a role in your Personal Branded Marketing, it's time to put it all together into an action plan.

Let's recap the elements of your marketing:

Blog
Facebook
LinkedIn
Twitter
YouTube
Biznik
Any other trade specific platform that you feel will benefit you.

The first step is to put together your Blog – or the hub of your online marketing. I would suggest that you use Wordpress.org to set up a blog. NOT Wordpress.com, but Wordpress.org. The difference is that the preferred way is on your own domain and not on someone else's. You're first going to need a name for your blog, or site. I would recommend that you use your own name since this is about personal branding after all.
Depending on your name, you may have to use some variance of it in order to find something that nobody else is using. You can purchase your domain name from just about anyplace you want to for around $10 per year.

So you've got your domain name, now you're going to need to set up a hosting account with a hosting provider in order to host your site. I highly suggest HostGator.com just because they are inexpensive (about $5 per month) and their platform is easy to use and set up yourself.

You will need to find a Wordpress theme, or template, that you like and want to use. There are a gazillion of FREE themes available so just search for Free Wordpress Themes and grab the one you like best. You can then download it into your HostGator, or other hosting provider, platform.

There are also a gazillion videos on YouTube that will show you not only how to set it up with your hosting provider, but you'll also find videos that will teach you how to use Wordpress. I would suggest that you watch some of these videos and get very familiar with Wordpress because you will love it.

Your blog is going to be about what you personally want to be branding yourself as. For instant, let's say you own a landscaping business. You'll want your blog to be all about landscaping to position yourself as the EXPERT in landscaping for your specific marketplace.

You'll want to create short videos and articles about whatever your subject matter is that you are going to brand yourself under. (more on this shortly)

You can link all of your social media platforms to your blog so that your blog readers can also connect with you in social networks.

As part of you blog, you'll want to include some sort of 'Lead Capture Form'. This is basically a form that you will install on your blog to assist in building a database of potential clients or customers of your product(s) or service(s). I would suggest that you offer an incentive to your blog readers to get them to complete the form and give you their name, email address, and potentially their cellphone number. As a landscaper, you could offer a *FREE Guide on How and When to Plant Bulbs.* Then once they complete the form on your site, they receive the FREE guide.

This is basic marketing 101. If you think about the Law of Reciprocity; you give something of value to someone for free and they feel obligated to do something in return – give you their name and email address. Now you are on your way to building a database of potential clients or customers that you can market to on a regular basis.

And the FREE guide does not have to be a novel. Just a few pages is fine as long as you are including valuable information that your potential client or customer is going to want, then you have the perfect offer. If you don't think you can write the FREE guide, then you can always hire someone to do this for you. There are many places that you can find someone to do this for you. A local college, freelance writers, a talented high school student could even prepare this for you. You could even check out sites online to find a writer. Try, www.FIVERR.com. This site is loaded with people who will do practically anything for just $5. I am sure you can find a report writer here for $5.

OK…so now that you have your blog set up, have a FREE offer written, you're going to need an automatic follow up system – an auto-responder. This is the system that will automatically respond to the requests when someone wants your FREE guide, it will send it out to them, capture their information and store it for you in a database.

There are many such systems available so you can search online to find one that you feel comfortable with. I personally use Aweber.com. It's very flexible and easy to use.

Once your reader makes a request for your FREE information, the system will capture their information and send them the information and you can continue to market your product(s) or service(s) to this potential customer using the auto-responder for as long as you want to. I would suggest that you send this person an email at least once per month, but preferably once per week for a great campaign. You just write a few paragraphs about whatever your subject is; let's say you send out tips about landscaping or planting or even the best time to water, etc. Plug these short articles, or tips, into your auto-responder, choose when you want your database to receive them and you are done. The system then runs on autopilot and you have a hands-free marketing system.

Next is your Social Media branding. You should already have these platforms built and working for you. You just need to continue keeping them updated with fresh content and updates about you or your business.

We talked briefly about video and article marketing, but now is when we need to expound on it. Video is the 'HOTTEST' thing on the internet! When someone goes to a website today, they expect to see video. It's not unusual to see blogs with not much text but lots of video – they're more of a video blog.

Use what I am about to teach you and you will see great results very quickly. Sit down with a notepad and write down the five most often asked questions about you or your business. Once you have done that, then write down the top five questions that you think your clients or customers should be asking of you. You should now have ten different questions.

Record yourself on video answering these ten questions separately so that you have ten unique videos. Then title each video with the question. For example, *'How deep do I need to dig my hole when I and planting a tree in my yard?'* If this was one of your ten questions then this could be the title to one of your videos. Upload the video to your YouTube channel, which you should already have established from our discussion in Chapter 15. Complete the full description of your video in the description box and begin the description with the URL address of your blog, then go into the description of the video. *Example, http://yourname.com, preparing the ground to plant a tree by digging your hole and landscaping the area around the tree is not difficult if you follow these simple rules.*

This is short, to the point, and includes a few keywords related to the video. Then you can 'tag' your video with more keywords in the section called 'Tags'. Use keywords related to the video and to what you do to promote you and your business.

I would highly suggest that you just go to YouTube.com and do a search for 'How to upload video for SEO purposes.'

Now that you have your video uploaded into YouTube, you can also upload it to other online video directories. There are quite a few, DailyMotion, Vimeo, Blip.tv, Viddler, and many more. You can use a service such as TubeMogul.com to assist you in distributing your video across the web. The more places you can distribute, the more chances you have of someone being able to find your videos.

The same goes with article marketing. One idea is to transcribe your videos to create articles. Use keywords throughout your articles that describe you and your services. Just as you distributed your video, you want to distribute your articles. There are multiple article directories that you can find by just doing a search.

Earlier I mentioned that when you create your Lead Capture Form for your website, or blog, that you give your potential customer the option of giving you their cellphone number. This is so that you can add mobile marketing to your overall marketing mix. Statistics show that text messaging has a very high success rate. That is because almost everyone now has texting plans on their phone and almost all of us are using this feature. In fact, there are more texts being sent than there are actual calls being made.

Recent numbers show that if you were to send out 100 marketing messages via text, that 98% of them will be opened with the first 15 minutes of receiving the text and 17% - 28% of those receiving the text message will actually act on the message. THIS IS HUGE! I don't know of any other marketing platform that can boast those kind of results.

So, this is why you should not only work towards building an email database of potential clients or customers but also a mobile database. The best company that I have found to help in this is called Inbound Local – www.InboundLocal.com.

Now if you really want to be aggressive in your online marketing you can also create your own Podcast. A podcast is simply a way to create audio, or video, programming that can be syndicated across the internet for others to hear or view. Think about it this way. What if you had your own radio show or TV show about you or your business that people could tune into LIVE or at any other time that is convenient to them. Do you think this would help you get more business? If you do, then this is something you should consider. It's not hard to do and it's not expensive to do. There are many sites available to teach you exactly how to do this. I am not going to go into it here because it would be an entire book. If this is something you are interested in I would just suggest that you do some research to find out more and then make your final decision. A couple of good resources are BlogTalkRadio.com, Libsyn.com, and BibPodcast.com.

Now, in between all of what I have mentioned in this chapter are more detailed elements that can be used to tie all of your online marketing and personal branding together. But, I only wanted to give you and introduction to what all of this looks like.

It may seem overwhelming at first but as you begin to understand Main Street Marketing 3.0 tactics and strategies, your comfort level will change and for most people it will change rapidly.

The key to remember is that times have changed. The way we market our products and services is changing as well. If you don't get on board YOU WILL GET LEFT BEHIND! If you don't begin to adopt the principles and practices mentioned in this book, you will not be able to grow your business as you used to. And if you really think about it, YOU need to be doing this before your competition does!

So, take the time to put together your own personal Action Plan for you or your business and go for it!

Links and Resources

www.InboundMarketing.com - a great site where you can get mobile marketing.

www.mashable.com - a great blog to stay abreast on social media marketing.

www.Meetup.com - a very good place to find a local group that you can get involved in to learn and network.

www.60secondmarketer.com - an online magazine for marketers and a good place to get great ideas.

www.LocalBrandedMarketing.com - this is my company that works with small to medium sized businesses and professionals with digital marketing.

www.LocalBrandedU.com - a learning site for marketing and branding.

www.Wordpress.org - the best platform to use for your blog.

www.HostGator.com - a great hosting service to use to host your blog.

www.HubSpot.com - incredible resource to learn about Inbound Marketing.

www.MarketingProfs.com - Social Media Marketing tips.

www.technorati.com - real time blog search engine

www.MarketingSherpa.com - social networking research

www.PersonalBrandingBlog.com - Dan Schawbel's blog on personal branding.

www.PersonalBrandingMag.com - magazine on personal branding

www.youtube.com/user/personalbrandingblog - Personal Branding TV

www.ChrisBrogan.com - Chris Brogan's blog on marketing, branding, and more.

www.BlogTalkRadio.com - Podcasting platform and information

About the Author

Leon E. Spencer is a marketer at heart. He blogs about marketing, and advertising at: www.LeonSpencer.com and has a huge following especially with small to medium sized business owners and professionals.

With nearly 30 years of experience in marketing and advertising, Leon focuses mainly on helping the local business professional to position themselves as experts within their specific market. His training in digital and social media allows the small business professional the opportunity to compete with big business.

Leon teaches professionals how to use social media to build their personal brands and their businesses to reach levels of success that they've never before been able to achieve. In fact, he is one of the most highly ranked marketers in social media today!

You can find him on the web at:

Blog   www.LeonSpencer.com

Twitter   @leonespencer

Facebook   http://Facebook.com/leonespencer.marketing

LinkedIn   http://LinkedIn.com/in/leonespencer

YouTube   http://Youtube.com/leonespencer

www.ingramcontent.com/pod-product-compliance
Lightning Source LLC
Chambersburg PA
CBHW061025050326

40689CB00012B/2703